Picture Poems

Volume 1

Thomas G. Reischel

Word Art Publishing
9350 Wilshire Blvd
Suite 203, Beverly Hills, CA 90212
www.wordartpublishing.com
Phone: 1 (888) 614 - 1370

Published by Word Art Publishing

ISBN: 978-1-955070-70-6 (Hardcover)
ISBN: 978-1-955070-75-1 (Paperback)
ISBN: 978-1-955070-59-1 (eBook)

DEDICATION

· ·

To my loving wife, Karen, who has been my guiding light, and to all poetry lovers everywhere.

INTRODUCTION

· ·

This book is the first of three volumes of poetry, each containing a set of 50 photographs joined with 50 associated poems of various styles and formats. I have combined here my talents of photography and poetry, that I hope you enjoy reading and viewing as much as I enjoyed creating them. I can't wait to present them to you here. But first, I'll begin with a discussion of my purpose and a short poetry primer.

I believe that photography and poetry go together well. One form paints a visual picture while the other creates a poetic image. Together, the synergy becomes very powerful. At least, that is what I hope I have achieved here. This book contains both. All the photographs contained in this book were taken by the author and the poetry was also written by him.

The author resides in St. Paul, Minnesota, USA. The photos were all taken within the state. So, besides the esthetic journey, he hopes the book also provides the reader a bit of information about the place that is his home.

Besides the poem itself, the author will typically add author's notes. These notes generally try to provide three bits of information. First will be a comment about the poem itself. Second, a description of the poetic format is provided. Finally, the author may comment about the photograph. This is provided to be informational. It may be redundant or unnecessary for some. Those individuals can skip over what they want, part or even all of the notes. They are there for those who appreciate them.

So, this book is really meant for several types of readers. There will be those who merely want to see the photographs. I think that is wonderful, and hope that my photography is sufficiently good enough to satisfy their craving. Others will just like the poetry. Again, although I don't purport to be an expert, I hope that I have at least accomplished some success and have whetted their appetite for more. Some may want to focus on style and format, and I believe this book should appeal to them as well.

The chapters have been organized by the category of photograph for the picture lovers, then in alphabetical order of the poem's title. There are chapters with Animal/Wildlife, Birds, Flowers, Gardens, Sunrise and Sunsets to please the eye.

The author doesn't claim to be an authority in these areas, so please allow him a bit of poetic license.

For those, who are new to poetry, I need to give a bit of information that may help you understand poetry better. This is necessary because I refer to these standard forms of poetic schematics frequently within my author's notes. So this section is intended to help a reader grasp the references adequately, not be a detailed poetry education. This is fairly technical, but I'll try to explain it as simply as possible. I didn't invent this system; it has been around a long time. I am merely going to explain some of it to you here. Those who are already familiar can skip this part of the introduction, unless you feel you need a refresher.

Poetry comes in many styles and forms. My poems identify what the style it is meant to be. Let's start with a discussion of rhyme. Poems may or may not have rhyme. The rhyme is usually at the end of each line and is known as "end rhyme". If not at the end, it is known as "in-line rhyme". As you read my poetic descriptions, I may refer to the end rhymes in an alphanumeric code. For example, the first rhyming word in a poem is referred to as the "a" rhyme, and every line in the poem that rhymes with it is designated the letter "a". The second rhyme to occur would be identified as "b", the third as "c", and so on. The most common poem has 4 lines (a Quatrain). The most typical end rhyme schemes for a quatrain are:

    aabb (Coupled Rhyme)
    abab (Alternating Rhyme)
    abba (Enveloping Ryme)
    abcb (Skipping Rhyme)

Poems may contain a paragraph. These are known as stanzas. These Stanzas may contain the same rhyme or may vary. Here are examples of the rhyme scheme of a poem with two stanzas.

aabb baba (Here the rhyme was the same in both, but one was coupled while the other was alternating).

aabb ccdd (Here each stanza has two different coupled rhymes)

Poems may also contain one or more repeating rhyme. That means it has the same identical rhyme word. This is usually identified using a capital letter, like so

Abab Abab (Here I'm referring to the first line of each stanza)

It could also mean a complete repeating line or refrain. That would be identified in the author's notes.

Poems may also have varying numbers of lines. Here is a list of the most common:

Couplet: 2 Lines
Tercet: 3 Lines
Quatrain: 4 lines
Quintet: 5 Lines
Septet: 6 Lines

Poems can also mix stanza styles. For example, a Sonnet usually contains 3 quatrains and a couplet (14 total lines).

Poems also may contain a structured syllable count. This establishes the rhythm at which the poem is read. This is known as meter. Typically these are paired in sets of two, known as a foot. There is a name for each type of meter, as follows.

Two syllables - Monometer (one foot)
Four syllables - Dimeter (two Feet)
Six syllables - Trimeter (three feet)
Eight syllables - Tetrameter (four feet)
Ten syllables - Pentameter (five feet)
Twelve syllables - Hexameter (six feet)
Fourteen syllables - Heptameter (seven feet)
Sixteen Syllables - Octameter (eight feet)

The ones most common or frequently used are tetrameter and pentameter.

The most complex poetic concept focuses around syllable accents, whether they are hard or soft, and how they are linked together. The most common of these are iambic and the trochaic (trochee) meters. As you speak a word, there is an accent on each syllable that results in either a soft or a hard sound. For example the word cowboy puts the hard accent on the first syllable – **COW**boy. The word police, puts the hard accent on the second syllable – po**LICE**. How you string words together determines the type of meter. Iambic meter alternates soft -hard, soft- hard. For example, Shakespeare's famous words –"To be or not to be" is iambic: to **BE** or **NOT** to **BE**. But the second half is not iambic – **THAT** is the **QUES**tion. Iambic is frequently defined as da-Dum, da-DUM type meter, where each da-Dum is a poetic foot. Therefore, iambic pentameter would carry a meter of: da-**DUM**, da-**DUM**, da-**Dum**, da-**DUM**, da-**DUM**. Trochee is exactly the opposite of iambic, where each line starts with a hard syllable accent and ends with a soft. **TWIN**kle **TWIN**kle **LIT**tle **STAR** how **I** won**DER** what **YOU** are.

Well, that's about as deep as I want to get.

Hope you enjoy this first volume.

ACKNOWLEDGEMENTS

. . . .

I'd like to recognize and thank my understanding wife, Karen Lynne (Sweetnam) Reischel, for providing support by reading all my poems as they were created and making helpful suggestions, as well as being the final editor. I'd also like to thank all my FanStory friends and fans who also helped and encouraged me. Finally, the staff at Word Art Publishing who provided their valuable assistance, especially Beau Brandon whose patience and persuasion over several years has gotten me here. Thank you all for your time and effort. For without it, this book could never have been possible.

TABLE OF CONTENTS

CHAPTER 1: ANIMALS/ WILDLIFE

. . . .

To the poet, wildlife presents a wonderful palette on which to paint poetic pictures of their antics and the moods that they create in the viewer while being observed.

They are wonderful subjects to photograph, whether they are: deer, squirrels, buffalo, horses, fish, monkeys, or whatever. They may be in the wild or in a zoo; in a forest or a lake. No matter where they are found, they are always interesting.

Poem #1:

CHIPMUNK
(A Rispetto with closing Envoi)

Those chubby cheeks that hold the seed,
A fuzzy face soon raids the stash.
He pilfers grain the birdies need,
This little guy's manners, so brash.

He scampers fast on tiny feet
While searching for a tasty treat.
An acrobatic climbing chum,
Who gobbles each and every crumb

The squirrels and chipmunks take their share,
But I don't care!

Whenever I load the bird feeder, the chipmunks and squirrels come to take their share. I don't mind. They are so cute and it's fun to watch their antics. Of course they make a mess. But everything seems to work out.

This poem is a Rispetto.

The Rispetto is a classic Italian form consisting of only 8 lines divided into two quatrains. The meter is iambic tetrameter: daDUMdaDUMdaDUMdaDUM. The distinguishing characteristic of this form is that the rhyme scheme changes from abab alternate-line rhyming in stanza one to ccdd couplet rhyming in the second.

I added a closing Envoi, which is a short stanza at the end of a poem used either to address an imagined or actual person, or (as in this case) comment on the preceding body of the poem.

The author took the accompanying photograph of his backyard birdfeeder on June 9, 2013.

Poem #2:

DEER IN THE GRASS
(Quatrains)

A deer was in the tall grass
As I walked along the shore.
'Cross the pond, it made a pass.
Couldn't ask for any more.

I had my trusty Kodak
So I caught it on my lens
Then it turned its timid back
And faded into the fens.

But it had nothing to fear!
That spooked little white-tailed deer.

While Camping this deer crossed my path at Lake Elmo Park Reserve in Minnesota

Quatrains with abab rhyming, Rhymed couplet. Syllable count 7 for the poem.

Fens are low-land swampy areas.

Spooked is frightened.

Author's photograph, taken May 25, 2013.

Poem #3:

ENJOY THE KOI
(Mixed Meter Quatrains)

I enjoy all the Koi
That swim in shallow pools.
They bring a bit of sunshine
In the shadows dark and cool.

They move about the pond
In groups of curiosity.
This one white, that one gold,
A black one then makes three.

I see so many in the pools.
They gather together in schools.
Colors flash as they flit around,
Leaving impressions most profound.

If you stick in a finger ,
Thinking it's a worm to eat,
The whole school will linger.
Remove it, and they'll retreat.

Such colorful little torpedoes
That add to the watery hues,
Have flashes of orange and indigos
That will chase away any blues.

Koi are colorful relatives of the Gold Fish that grow larger and come in several colors.

Just simple unmetered Quatrains. Mixed abcb and abab rhyming.

This photograph was taken by the author at the Japanese Garden at Como Park in St. Paul, Minnesota.

Poem #4:
STARTLED SQUIRREL
(A Lune)

Flakes freak startled squirrel
snowy nose
frowns in panic pose

This squirrel seems puzzled by the clump of snow on its nose.

Freak used as a verb as in: "You freak me out".

This poem is a Lune.

The Lune is also known as the American Haiku. It was first created by the poet Robert Kelly and was a result of Kelly's frustration with English haiku. After much experimentation, he settled on a 13-syllable, self-contained poem that has 5 syllables in the first line, 3 syllables in the second line and 5 syllable in the final line.

Unlike haiku, there are no other rules. No need for a cutting word. Rhymes are fine; subject matter is open. While there are less syllables to use, this form has a little more freedom.

Author's photograph taken on his back porch in February 2013.

Poem #5:

THE BUCK
(Quatrain)

He stood there in that stately stance
Displaying that velvety valance,
And as he stood there in that pose,
He blithely licked his big black nose.

A simple little Children's Poem

The poem is a single Quatrain written with aabb rhyme scheme. The syllable count is 8 (Tetrameter).

This is a Photograph I actually took from my convertible as I was driving through Union Cemetery on the East side of St. Paul, Mn. in July, 2012 on the way to visit my dad's grave.

This poem is totally inspired by the photo

CHAPTER 2: BIRDS

Birds are magnificent in their varying size, color of plumage, diversity of habits and habitats. Creatures of the air, trees, grasses and waters that never cease to fascinate. Great subjects for the poet's muse and the photographer's eye. Whether at the feeder or in the air they brighten our days with action and sound. They may delight us or awe us. Still or in motion, they are wonderful creatures that grace our lives.

Poem #6:

AMERICAN KESTREL

When you think red, white, and blue
Does a bird thought come to you?

If it didn't, I won't tell.
Since, it flustered me as well.
That's the colors on this bird.
So, let me pass the word
That it's about a Kestrel.

Not an Eagle or an Owl,
It is not a water fowl,
As this Raptor's pretty face
Has some patriotic grace.

It's a little bird of prey
That helps keep the mice away.

With those colors in its wings,
As I think about these things,
We should find a good minstrel.
Make a song about Kestrel
During games, everyone sings.

The American Kestrel is a pretty, tiny raptor that has very patriotic colors

This poem is no particular format. It has a syllable count of 7 and a variable rhyme scheme.

This picture was taken by the author in September 2012 at a Raptor show.

Poem #7:

CARDINAL RULES

Awoke to Cardinal song.
Its tune was sweet,
Notes were long,
A morning greet.
Came along,
A pleasant tweet.
Then it's gone!

That red bird
Started the day
With sweet joy.
I'd have to say.
Began it with
A song of praise.
We all should learn birdie ways!

Just enjoy this feathered guest
With an Angel's voice,
Scarlet plumes,
That mates for life.
Serenades
Its pretty wife.
A bird Best!

I actually did wake up this morning to Cardinal song. Had to pen this.

This is a tumbling Whitney (if there can be such a thing).

A Whitney normally has a fixed syllable count of 3434347. I turned that upside down twice. So, this Tumbling Whitney has this syllable structure. 7434343 3434347 7434343.

Whitney's don't require a rhyme scheme. I added rhyme, but not to a fixed scheme.

This photograph is from the Author's collection. I captured it sitting on my back deck's railing eating seed my wife had set out. Got a picture of his pretty wife too.

Poem #8:

GREAT HORNED OWL
(A Rondeau Cinquain)

Great Horned Owl, predator of night,
With silent stealth and searing sight,
Fierce hunters in the nighttime skies
Whose quiet wings bring quick surprise.
Small things beware when they take flight.

There's instant death when talons bite,
As owls swoop down from hidden height,
Ravenous hunger in keen eyes

Great Horned Owl, predator of night,
With silent stealth and searing sight,
Fierce hunters in the nighttime skies

But when dawn breaks, they soon alight
To roost and doze in bright daylight.
At dusk begins distinguished cries,
"Hoo Hoo HOO HOO" their lullabies
Sounds that fill the quiet twilight

Great Horned Owl, predator of night,
With silent stealth and searing sight,
Fierce hunters in the nighttime skies
Whose quiet wings bring quick surprise.
Small things beware when they take flight.

The Great Horned Owl is a fascinating raptor. According to Wikipedia, the Great Horned Owl, (Bubo virginianus), also known as the Tiger Owl, is a large owl native to the Americas. The combination of the species' bulk, prominent ear-tufts and barred plumage distinguishes it. Since owls are perhaps the main predator of crows and their young, crows sometimes congregate from considerable distances to mob owls and caw angrily at them. Owls have spectacular binocular vision, allowing them to pinpoint prey and see in low light. The eyes of a Great Horned Owl are immobile within their circular bone sockets. As a result, instead of turning its eyes, an owl must turn its whole head, The neck is capable of rotating a full 270 degrees. Owls also have approximately 300 pounds per square inch (PSI) of crushing power in their talons. Almost all prey is killed with the owl's talons, often instantly. According to one author, "Almost any living creature that walks, crawls, flies, or swims, except the large mammals, is the great horned owl's legitimate prey". The Great Horned is also a natural predator of prey two to three times heavier than itself such as porcupines, marmots and skunks. According to the Cornell Lab of Ornithology, the Great Horned Owl is the only regular avian predator of skunks. Birds also compose a large portion of a Great Horned Owl's diet, ranging in size from kinglets to Great Blue Herons and young swans. Regular avian prey includes woodpeckers, grouse, crows, pigeons, herons, gulls, quail, and turkey. Even cats and dogs my become prey.

This poem is a Rondeau Cinquain.

A rondeau (plural rondeaux) is a form of medieval and Renaissance French poetry that utilize a repeated line, or lines, know as a refrain. In larger rondeau variants, each of the structural sections may consist of several verses, although the overall sequence of sections remains the same. Variants include the Rondeau Tercet, where the refrain consists of three verses, the Rondeau Quatrain, where it consists of four (and, accordingly, the whole form of sixteen), and the rondeau cinquain, with a refrain of five verses (and a total length of 21), which becomes the norm in the 15th century. In the Rondeau Cinquain the rhyme sequence is:

A1,A2,B1,B2,A3 - aab - A1,A2,B1 - aabba - A1,A2,B1B2,A3, where the capital letters represent the repeated refrains.

This photograph of the Great Horned Owl was taken by the author himself at Fort Snelling State Park along the river bottoms of the Mississippi River.

Poem #9:

OWL'S STARE

(An Octogram)

><...><
Are there looks that can replace
The Owl's stare?
Huge eyes within a feathered face,
You must beware!
That friendly face contains a beak,
He'll warn you with a piercing shriek.
Be careful! If you see it glare,
The Owl's stare.

><
If you're beguiled by owlish grace,
Then have a care.
Be wary of a nightly chase,
If you're a hare.
Hesitate once, rabbit's surprise,
Death is looking you in the eyes.
Captures food with distinctive flair,
The Owl's stare.

Owls have amazing eyes. But to small animals, their stare is lethal.

An Octogram Poem based on the Photograph

Syllable count is 84848884, repeat on second stanza.

Rhyme scheme: aBabccbB ababddbB, where B repeats same text.

No more than 16 lines.

The Author's photograph taken during a presentation by the Raptor center.

Poem #10:

REDWINGED BLACKBIRD
(Quatrains)

I hear a Redwinged Blackbird's cry,
And watch it sail through the tall grass.
It stops to watch the world go by.
Lets out a sharp scree as I pass.

It likes to sit upon a reed,
Then takes wing with its colors shown.
I marvel at its agile speed,
And markings that are its alone

Just out in Nature. Redwinged Blackbirds love the reeds along shorelines of lakes and ponds.

Two rhyming quatrains. Syllable count: 8. Rhyme scheme: abab

Took this picture of a Redwinged Blackbird in flight at Battle Creek Park in May 2012.

Poem #11:

TREE SWALLOWS
(A Triolet Poem)

Tree swallows find a numbered nest
To make a home and raise their young,
Upon the roof, I see one rest.
Tree swallows find a numbered nest
To fly to in their daily quest
To share with those they live among.
Tree swallows find a numbered nest
To make a home and raise their young.

I found a field with tree swallows in their nests while I was camping this weekend.

This poem is a Triolet Poem. Triolet is a poem of only eight lines with a rhyme scheme abaaabab. The fourth and seventh lines are the same exact line as the first. The eighth line is the same exact line as the second.

This photograph is one of the author's collection taken with his Sony Alpha camera Memorial Day weekend while camping at Lake Elmo county park in Minnesota on May 27, 2013.

Poem #12:

WHEN EAGLE'S EYES LOOK
(A Rondeau Poem)

When Eagle's eyes look on their prey
There's very few that get away.
Once fixed within that icy stare,
It spells the doom of hound or hare
On raptor's rav'nous hunting day.

Sharp talons pierce as victims bray.
They soon consume what e'er they slay,
Or feed it to an eaglet pair,
When Eagle's eyes look.

The sun may save, some sages say.
High bird-borne shadows can betray
The present peril to beware.
If lucky victims stay aware,
Then fate may turn another way,
When Eagle's eyes look.

What is more spectacular than an Eagle landing. Its very size is impressive. Then there is that razor beak and sharp, powerful talons.

This poem is a Rondeau.

Rondeau is a fixed form of poetry. It is often used in light or witty poems. It often has fifteen octo - or decasyllabic lines with three stanzas. It usually only has two rhymes (a & b) used in the poem. A word or words from the first part of the first line are used as a refrain ending the second and third stanzas. The rhyme scheme, then, is;

aabba aabR aabbaR.

The format can carry any type of meter or syllable count, as long as it follows a fixed pattern.

Photograph by the Author

CHAPTER 3: FLOWERS

For overall beauty, it is hard to beat the flower. Such variety of size, shape and color is a poet's as well as photographer's dream. Some have been beautifully cultured and domesticated. Others are wildflowers. There's even the lowly weed. All of them are unique and exquisite. This chapter gives the reader a sampling of each.

Poem #13:

ANEMONE
(Whitneys - 2)

Pretty white
Anemone,
Broad petals
That mimic wings
Of angels,
Gently settles
In a sanctifying sight.

Such beauty
Within garden
Soothes my soul.
Nature's bounty
In the sun
Makes me extol
It's white wonders with great glee.

These lovely white flowers are Anemones. There are several varieties, and I'm not sure which these are. They could either be the Japanese Anemone, or the Snowdrop Anemone. In any case, I spotted them at the Lake Harriet Rose Gardens. I loved their broad petals that I described here as Angel wings. They almost look like Butterflies.

This poem is a Whitney. Two, actually.

A Whitney is a poem that has a set format of 3/4/3/4/3/4/7. I've done this one in two Whitneys to make two stanzas in Whitney format. I've also added rhyming which is not a requirement of this style, but not a specific scheme.

This photograph was taken by the author himself.

Poem #14:

BIRD-FOOT TREFOIL
(Quatrains)

Little yellow flowers
That dot across the glade,
Kissed by summer showers,
Or hidden in the shade.

They easily take root
In damp and sandy soil.
Named after a bird's foot,
And called a Trefoil.

But you must be careful,
If given to a friend,
Their meaning is awful.
Revenge is what you send.

A wildflower, the pretty yellow Birds-foot Trefoil. I see these growing wild everywhere. Frequently with clover in open fields and shade. In Europe they used to be called "Butter and Eggs" for their yellow color. The leaves come in three - thus "tre"foil, and the shape is like a bird's foot. In flower language, this is one of the few flowers with a negative connotation, meaning Revenge. Source: Wikipedia.

This poem is a set of three rhymed quatrains (A poem with four lines). The rhyme scheme is abab. The syllable count is 6.

This picture was taken by the author in Maplewood, Minnesota.

Poem #15:

BLUES AND HUES
(A Corniced Overlap)

I love this blue and colored hue
Upon the pebbled path that grew
Hither, where I will walk.
The beauty makes me gawk,
And oft' yearn to come back again.

Yon leaves, the joy of noblemen.
The green that bleeds maroon, Amen!
Such lovely tinted prayer,
Placed there with loving care.
Amazing blend of pure delight.

Yet 'tis the pink that draws thy sight.
'Twas 'cause its petals shine so bright.
Amongst the scattered green,
It's sitting so serene,
To bring forth spicy splash of joy.

Tranquility that plants deploy
Make merry settings I enjoy.
Whilst out in nature's sphere,
I truly like it here.
Shall never take for granted.

Thus, flora was planted
To keep us enchanted.
I love this blue and colored hue
Upon the pebbled path that grew
Hither, where I will walk.

This poem was inspired by this photograph. I tried to bring out the blend of the greens, blues, and pink that I spotted along a garden path. Some of the leaves are tinged with maroon. Such diversity blends beautifully, and made me wax a bit Elizabethan.

I just created this poem's format on my own. I don't know if there is such a layout that already exists. If so, let me know. I am calling it a Corniced Overlay, due to the structure of the rhyme scheme. Like a stone wall made of bricks that are similar, there is a unique capstone, or cornice, that is different from the rest. Each stanza has 4 lines laid out in a classical aabb scheme, but the fifth line is different. Thus the cornice. However, that unique last line becomes the rhyme for the first two lines of the next stanza. Thus the overlay. I used 5 stanzas here, but it could have been any number. However, the last three lines of the last stanza repeat the first three of the first stanza. For this poem then, the rhyme scheme was:

AABbc ccdde eeffg gghhi iiABB,

where the capital letters are the repeated lines.

There is also a fixed syllable count of

8/8/6/6/8 in every stanza, except for the last,

which inverts it, to

6/6/8/8/6,

Due to the structure required to repeat the first three lines. I hope that makes sense.

This photograph was taken by the author at the Como Park Conservatory in St. Paul, Minnesota.

Poem #16:

BRILLIANT YELLOW STAR
(A Quatern)

When brilliant yellow stars shine bright,
They are not always in the sky,
As some create a floating sight,
On lily pads that grow nearby.

You may find sweet serenity
When brilliant yellow stars shine bright.
Wishes become reality,
Although it isn't really night.

On water standing so upright,
An amazing aquatic plant,
When brilliant yellow stars shine bright,
There's a tendency to enchant.

Make a wish on one when you find
A brilliant glow of pure delight,
In the Creator's pure design,
When brilliant yellow stars shine bright.

This amazing little aquatic plant that looks like a twinkling star, or even a starfish, is actually a flower called a Nymphoides Crenata. A true water nymph that can be found in bogs, ponds, aquariums, and even some wishing wells. Its leaves resemble lily pads. It has long underwater roots and floating leaves. It is typically yellow, but white ones are known as water snowflakes. Each flower lasts only one day, but the plant produces many more as the roots spread ultimately providing a blizzard of yellow. It blooms from early spring until the first hard frost. Source: Wikipedia

This poem is a Quatern.

The Quatern is a French form of poetry that is composed of four quatrains, (four-line stanzas). It is similar to the Kyrielle and other French poems, in that it has a repeated refrain. The first line of the poem, ripples through each succeeding stanza like water flowing down a hill. Unlike other French forms, it doesn't have to rhyme--there is no rhyme scheme specified. Similar to other French forms of poetry, the Quatern consists of lines with eight syllables each, and has no required meter.

Even though they do not have to rhyme or follow a specific meter, I have chosen to write my Quatern poem in iambic tetrameter with a rhyme scheme of: Abab, cAca, adAd, eaeA, where the first and third lines of each stanza rhyme and where the second and fourth lines of each stanza rhyme, and the A represents the Refrain line.

This photograph was taken by the author in the floating garden surrounding the Como Conservatory in St. Paul, Minnesota.

Poem #17:

FLEABANE, NOT DAISIES
(6/8 Verse)

Fleabane are not Daisies,
But they sure seem to want to be.
Pretty in the sunlight,
Or in the shade between the trees.
Loaded with much pollen,
So they're quite popular with bees.
Considered nasty weeds,
They have nothing to do with fleas.
Often find clumps of them
Blowing softly in summer breeze.
They're so misunderstood,
These tiny flowers surely please
Lovers of wildflowers
Who may lack Botany degrees.

Another in my Wildflower series

Fleabane is a wildflower that is often mistaken for Daisies due to their yellow center and white petals, or for the Aster which has similar petals, but is larger. This hearty wildflower is small and has many narrow petals. It grows well almost anywhere. It has lots of pollen but very little nectar, so bees love it. It is a small flower that is seldom larger than 1 inch wide. It can have other colors than white, but white is the most common in the wild. The name Fleabane is derived from an old wives tale that the dried stalks, when burned created a smoke that chased away fleas. This was disproven centuries ago.

This poem is written with a continuous 6/8 syllable count' Its rhyme scheme is abcb.

This photograph was taken by the author on July 12, 2013 in Maplewood, Minnesota

Poem #18:

PANSIES
(A Sonniolet)

Those tiny seeds I placed deep in the ground
Were watered all freely and left to grow.
Then nurtured soil weekly to keep them sound,
Those tiny seeds I placed deep in the ground.
I dreamt they'd be the best flowers around.
Those tiny seeds I placed deep in the ground
Were watered all freely and left to grow.

Then from the fertile earth a shoot did sprout,
A delicate sprig with a promise of joy.
I tended the dirt to keep the weeds out,
Then from the fertile earth a shoot did sprout,
A wondrous miracle without a doubt,
A beautiful blossom, each to enjoy.
Then from the fertile earth a shoot did sprout,
A delicate sprig with a promise of joy.

Now blessed with a dash of white, yellow, blue,
The color burst forth from my new pansies.
They proudly displayed color, tint, and hue,
Now blessed with a dash of white, yellow, blue.
With smashing smile, it's beaming right at you,
They flash pizzazz like little dandies.
Now blessed with a dash of white, yellow, blue,
The color burst forth from my new pansies.

I cherish each little tinted treasure.
Their graceful presence gives me much pleasure

A story about Pansies: from planting, to growth, and finally to bursting colorful blooms.

What I did here was create a Sonniolet. Its takes the conventional Sonnet format of three quatrains and rhyming couplet in iambic pentameter, and replaces it with three Triolets and rhyming couplet. Still in iambic pentameter. Triolets are usually in tetrameter. So both forms have been slightly modified to create this format.

This is a photograph that I took in March, when I was in Vegas,

Poem #19:

POOF!

Just a puff
of a brisk breeze,
or sometimes
a heavy sneeze,
sets in flight
this fragile fluff.
Seeds of yellow explosion

Springtime guest.
Weed or flower?
Sun shower
provides the best
conditions
to grow this pest.
Proud pioneer of the lawn!

Often fought,
pulled or poisoned.
Left unwatched,
Its seeds will blow
fertile fluff.
Unheralded!
Indomitable Flower!

Poof!

Wishing for spring. Dandelions are welcome!

This is a Whitney poem I slightly modified by adding the exclamations in front and back. A whitney has a set format of 3/4/3/4/3/4/7. I've done three stanzas in whitney format. I've also added rhyming, but not a specific scheme.

This was inspired by Whitneys written by both Adewpearl and Gungalo. Thought I'd do one too.

The picture is my own photograph taken at Maplewood nature center in June 2012.

Poem #20:

THISTLE WEED
(Free Verse)

I get the point
of
Thistle,
as it
screams
"Don't touch me".
While it draws you to purple flowers,
heed the warning,
or
you might bleed.

It
has a noble beauty
as it seems
so
straight and tall
but
it comes
with cutting edges
and
they
aren't friendly
at all.

This is Bull Thistle. One of several varieties of thistle with a purple flower, it grows taller than surrounding vegetation and has very recognizable sharp barbs. It is a wildflower, but is definitely considered a weed. The thorns are a method to protect it from being eaten by herbivores. According to Wikipedia, in heraldry, the Thistle has been a national symbol of Scotland and a strong Celtic symbol of strength, as well as birth. Its image was used on silver coins and there is an Order of the Thistle in Scotland as well. The thistle flower attracts butterflies and Goldfinches. When God expelled Adam and Eve from the Garden of Eden, He said "...thorns and thistles shall I bring forth..." (Genesis 3:17-18). Source: Wikipedia

This poem is a Free Verse that does have some incidental rhyming, but no formal structure.

This picture was taken by the author June 12,2013.

Poem #21:

YELLOW ROSE
(A 1962 Poem)

FLOWER,
Captivating sight seen any hour,
With fragrance that's so sweet.
A Treat!

SCENT,
Fragrance drifts to nose, rose gift is lent,
As fumes delight so well.
Sweet smell!

PETAL,
No true artistic soul would settle
For lesser floral sight.
So bright!

YELLOW,
With highlights of a radiant glow,
Such as Angel's halo.
Bravo!

ROSE,
The champion at flower shows.
Its beauty, very fine.
Divine!

I recently went to the Lake Harriet Rose Garden in Minneapolis, Minnesota, that has an amazing display of several species of rose. This yellow one is just one. I will likely feature others in the coming days.

The Rose has been a venerated flower since the beginning of recorded time. They have become ancient symbols of love and beauty. There are over 100 varieties. They can grow singly, in clusters, as a bush, or in climbing vines. Very fragrant, the yellow rose is associated with sunshine, happiness, and friendship.

This poem is a new style poem that Ritchie, 9999pool introduced us to. This Child Four or "1962" format was developed by Fanstorian Ann aka ann marie mazz.

It has a fixed syllable count per line: 1-9-6-2, where

Line 1: 1 syllable

Line 2: 9 syllables

Line 3: 6 syllable

Line 4: 2 syllables

no stanza limit

rhyming is optional

This photograph was taken by the author.

CHAPTER 4: GARDEN

· ·

What is a garden, but a place of beauty crafted by the hand of mankind? It is a sanctuary, a place of solitude and contemplation, and a place to go and marvel at the colors that abound. Each garden is a masterpiece in its own right. Most have paths and places to sit. Some may have water in pools, fountains, or ponds. All are to be viewed and appreciated. They are natural magnets for the poet and the photographer. This chapter is meant to give a flavor of some.

Poem #22:

COME TO MY GARDEN
(Faux Limerick)

Come to my garden and walk with me.
So many colorful sights to see,
With lovely marbled path,
Plants in a floating bath.
Oh, what a wonderful place to be!

A shot of the Sunken Garden area at the Como Park Conservatory. There is a lovely path to walk through this lovely serene setting. It is always warm, colorful, and inviting at any time of year. A real treat to visit on a cold Minnesota winter day.

Faux Limerick: five lines, Syllable count 9/9/6/6/9. Rhyme scheme: aabba

This photograph was taken by the author himself.

Poem #23:

FLOWER GARDEN
(A Rispetto Poem)

Just take me to a garden,
Where the pretty flowers grow,
As all those colors beckon,
In a dazzling floral show.

And let me sit amongst them
To see each petal and stem,
On a lovely marble bench.
What memories they'll entrench.

Inspired by the beauty of this lovely spot as captured in this picture. Within the Rose Garden a marble bench beckons tired visitors to sit among the lush beauty.

This poem is a Rispetto.

A Rispetto is an Italian poetic format consisting of two quatrains with a changing rhyme scheme. In the first quatrain it is abab rhyming. In the second is aabb rhyming.

For this poem I chose the syllable count to be 7.

The author took this picture at Lake Harriet Rose Garden in Minneapolis.

Poem #24:

GOD'S GARDEN
Ternet (Terza Rima Sonnet)

God's garden has a background that's colored green,
Pastel tinted flowers, with a place to sit.
Prettiest corner spot that I've ever seen!

Many is the day I'd like to sit a bit,
Where dappled sunlight chases flirting shadows
Past canopy of leaves hanging over it.

Time's gainfully spent in idyllic meadows
With flowered scents from blooms sweetly filling air
Whose palette matches colors of the rainbows.

Among many things that lend a vibrant flair
Are places full of such quiet dignity,
Where rejuvenation transforms any care.

Such a place of peace will set your spirit free,
To keep a weary soul tuned with Deity.

A beautiful garden spot brings a feeling of peace and serenity that helps to synchronize a soul with the vibrations of the Creator.

This poem is a Ternet, which is a hybrid of two styles - a Terza Rima and a Sonnet. A TERNET has the syllable count and rhyme scheme of a Terza Rima (11 lines,11 syllables in each line, and rhyme scheme aba,bcb,cdc,dd).

A Sonnet has lines (14) of 3 quatrains and 2 rhyming couplets.(Italian Sonnet has 11 syllables each line).

Thus, a TERNET blends the two and must have 14 lines with 11 syllables in each line and the rhyme scheme as

aba,bcb,cdc,ded,ee.

I struggled whether two have 12 lines without spaces plus the couple, or to separate the tercets and couplets. I decided to retain the integrity of the tercets in mine, as the other way seems to lose the character of the Terza Rima.

This photograph was taken be the author himself.

Poem #25:

JAPANESE GARDEN
(A Free Style Poem)

I came upon a garden.
One like they have
in Japan.

It really left me
speechless,
As I saw
The sights it had.

Forget about clocks,
As you watch
the mystic spot.

You'll lose
your sense of time,
while
earthy mystery unlocks,
in primal patterns
of stones,
with marbled history,

as written in the rocks.

Burnished
By the wind,

Sanded striations
of white,
and gray,
and rusty brown
blocks.

They lurk in a basin.
Reflections on the surface play.

Inverted images,
mirroring
their master's mood.
Projecting
something good,

A feeling understood
Within our soul.

Tranquility greets the eye,
where
Waterfalls whisper
their ancient rocky lullaby,
while water
trickles down
to rule
the pool.

I stand by
a twisted Juniper.
Pruned
And sculpted to please
Mankind.

Transfixed
And speechless.

This is a waterfall located in the Ordway Japanese Garden at Como Park in Minnesota that I recently visited.

A simple Free Style poem. No formal structure, some rhyme and no formal scheme.

This picture was taken by the Author on September 7, 2013.

Poem #26:

SILENT RAPTURES
(An Octogram)

Behold the splendors of the Zen,
Silent raptures.
Quiet serenity within
Peace that captures,
The very beat of nature's heart
With every blended innate part ,
Using rocks and trees for structure,
Silent raptures.

Where plants and water both abide,
Winning juncture's.
Elemental balance provides
Mystic mixtures,
Taught to us by the Japanese,
In gardens that are meant to please
The eye with natural sculptures,
Silent raptures.

This is a picture from the Ordway Japanese Garden at Como Park in St. Paul, Minnesota. Japanese gardens use organized nature to express serenity and create a Zen experience, which are feelings of silent rapture within as you contemplate the beauty.

This poem is an Octogram.

The Octogram is a style of poetry invented by Fanstorian Sally Yocom (S.Yocom). It consists of two stanzas of eight lines each, with a very specific syllable count and rhyme scheme.

Syllable count is 84848884, repeat on second stanza.

Rhyme scheme: aBabccbB ababddbB, where B repeats same text repeated.

No more than 16 lines.

This photograph was taken by the author himself.

Poem #27:

STAIRWAY TO HEAVEN
(A Free verse Poem)

As
I stepped
into the room,
I was immediately
engulfed
in warmth and humidity.
Surrounded
by lush green plants
that towered above me.

When
I looked up,
I saw green spires
assending to the heights,
and
I held my breath,
and stood there
in Awe.

It was a Minnesota winter in February. The temperature outside was 12 degrees F. I went to the Margery McNeely Conservatory at Como Zoo in St. Paul, Minnesota.

This poem expresses what my feelings were as I entered the tropical Fern Room. It was hot and humid, with huge ferns and palms reaching 100 feet to the dome of the building.

I will be adding this to my book of picture poems. Picture Poems are poems that are inspired by the photograph, and wouldn't exist except for that picture.

Poem #28:

REFLECTIONS ON THE WATER
(A Petrarchan Sonnet)

On water, fine reflections reign supreme,
With mirrored images that float in sight,
Of colors - purple, green, with red and white.
This tableau that sits simply so serene
Beside a building looking most pristine,
Through shining glass-clad windows, such delight
That fills the mind with thoughts of fancy flight,
A vision placed as if it were a dream.

Yet, were the water to be swiftly drained,
Too soon would these reflections disappear.
Might quickly kill the plants and mar our cheer.
The elegance of art would be profaned.
So, let us pray those waters stay in place,
This circumstance must never be the case.

Oh the beauty of reflections on water. This one is a floating garden, man made. It is next to the Como Park Conservatory.

This poem is a Petrarchan Sonnet.

Petrarch developed the Italian sonnet pattern, which is known to this day as the Petrarchan sonnet. Francesco Petrarca (Petrarch in English; July 20, 1304 -July 19, 1374) was a scholar and poet in Renaissance Italy. Petrarch's sonnets were admired and imitated throughout Europe during the Renaissance and became a model for lyrical poetry. The original Italian sonnet form divides the poem's 14 lines into two parts, the first part being an octave and the second being a sestet. The rhyme scheme for the octave is typically:

a b b a a b b a.

The sestet is more flexible. In Italian sonnets in English,

c d d c e e and c d c d e e are most used.

The entire poem is written in iambic pentameter.

The octave and sestet have special functions in a Petrarchan Sonnet. The octave's purpose is to introduce a problem, express a desire, reflect on reality, or otherwise present a situation that causes doubt or conflict within the speaker. It usually does this by introducing the problem within its first quatrain (unified four-line section) and developing it in the second. The beginning of the sestet is known as the volta, and it introduces a pronounced change in tone in the sonnet; the change in rhyme scheme marks the turn. The sestet's purpose as a whole is to make a comment on the problem or to apply a solution to it. Source: Wikipedia.

This photograph was taken by the author himself.

CHAPTER 5: INSECTS

. . . .

Insects can be beautiful, as the butterfly; strange, like the spider or scorpion; or ugly, like the stink bug. You wouldn't think there's much to be poetic about in this group, but maybe that's not true. The author hopes this chapter will give a better appreciation for the topic and the creatures that are its subject matter.

Poem #29:

BLACK AND YELLOW DRAGONFLY
(Free Style Verse)

A dragonfly
With a big white eye
Alights

A handsome fellow
Black and yellow
See through wings
Delicate things

I might mention
A dandelion in its sights
Seems to be the object of its attention

I ponder
And wonder
About its intention.

In a funny way
It seems to say

Open up
Buttercup
That I might sup
The nectar in your cup.
I'll lap it up

A dragonfly
With a big white eye
Alights

While out for a walk in the park with my wife, a dragonfly alighted nearby. I took its picture. It is so cute; I was inspired to write this little poem.

This dragon fly is named a Dot-tailed Whiteface, Leucorrhinia intacta. I think the name says it all.

This poem is free style, in that there is no formal structure. It does contain rhyme, but not to any fixed pattern.

I took this photograph on June 23, 2013 while on a walk with my wife at Battle Creek Park in Maplewood, Minnesota, a suburb of St. Paul.

Poem #30:

BROWN BUTTERFLY
(A Gertrude Poem)

I was walking, when I found, brown
Butterfly upon the ground, down
Where I could see its filigree, white against the sand.
It was sitting on the beach, but
It was slightly out of reach, what
Could I do, but simply view. I hadn't planned
To see such fuzzy wings like this,
That send a pulmonary bliss.
I will dance and I will prance, I'll even strut.
Oh what Fate! I just can't wait, when
I could show it to my mate. Then
With no clue, it quickly flew, right out of town.

This butterfly is called a Morning Cloak. Brown velvety wings, and a filigree of white lace around the wings, distinguish this beautiful insect.

This poem is a Gertrude Poem. A Gertrude poem is a poem with a very unique structure and tempo. It carried sets of three tercets with a syllable count of 8/8/11 for a minimum of 3 sets. I wrote it in 4 sets, making a minimum of 12 lines.

The rhyme scheme for this is: aabccbddceea.

The tempo is the most unique aspect of the poem. The rhythm goes like this, with da being unaccented and DUM being an accented syllable. The letters A, B, C show the rhyme pattern.

da da DUM da da da DUM da (A)

da da DUM da da da DUM da (A)

da da DUM da da da DUM da da da DUM (B)

da da DUM da da da DUM da (C)

da da DUM da da da DUM da (C)

da da DUM da da da DUM da da da DUM (B)

The photograph was taken by the author in Northern Minnesota, on the beach at Red Lake, in September 2012.

Poem #31:

DRAGONFLY
(Free Style)

I dance
the sky on
golden
gossamer wings,
That carry me across
the fields to play
on plants and flowers
along the way.

The sun
shines through my
crystal vanes
to speed me on,
and light the way
as I dance and dart
the day
away.

When I alight,

I pause,
hanging on,
as I apprise
what heaven has wrought
to dazzle all my eyes.

I lift
my dragon's tail,
in praise,
as I gaze
at the wonders
of the world.

You may think
this
a simple weed.

We're not agreed.

I can see
the unique pedigree,
for I have touched a thousand
in my day
and
find
no two the same

A Dragonfly has large multi-faceted compound eyes. A large dragon fly may have as many as 30,000 ommatida (lens cell) in their eye. They eat mosquitoes and can hover like a helicopter. They have flight speeds that can reach 60 MPH.

This poem is a Free Style Poem.

A Free Style poem is a subcategory of Free Verse poetry. It is unstructured with on specific meter, stanza length, number of lines or syllable count, but contains rhyme within it. Whereas Free Verse is unrhymed.

This is one of the author's photographs that he took in July 2012 along the Bruce Vento trail near downtown St. Paul, Minnesota.

Poem #32:

FLUTTER
(A Triolet Poem)

I watch them as they flutter by,
Their wings touched by the painter's brush.
Their color simply fills the sky.
I watch them as they flutter by,
Such dainty grace delights the eye,
Just sipping nectar, in no rush.
I watch them as they flutter by,
Their wings touched by the painter's brush.

Remembering Summer delights. A butterfly alights to sip the nectar of the flower.

This poem is a Triolet

A Triolet is a poem of only eight lines. The fourth and seventh lines are the same exact line as the first. The eighth line is the same exact line as the second. This one is done in iambic tetrameter with a rhyme pattern of ABaAabAB (where the capital letters are the repeated lines).

This photograph was taken by the Author in May, 2012.

Poem #33:

INSECT ON THE ROCKS
(An Essence Poem)

Turquoise damselfly, poise
Simple joys, each wing employs

A beautiful turquoise Damselfly sits on a rock. How pretty these delicate insects are. Similar to a Dragonfly, a Damselfly has one pair of wings, as opposed to two sets. It looks very much like a flying stick.

This is an Essence Poem.

An Essence Poem was created Emily Romano. It is a short and simple form that is meant to be expressive. Like the Japanese Haiku, it should express much in few words. The difference is that, this format encourages rhyming. It has two lines of strict structure, having a requirement of six syllables each. Each line must include in-line rhyme.

This photograph was taken at Lake Phalen in St. Paul, Minnesota in July of 2013.

Poem #34:

TAKING FLIGHT
(A Faux Limerick Poem)

When things take flight on filigreed wings,
The beauty takes hold of my heart strings.
Then as pure fancy flies
Right In front of my eyes,
my whole countenance joyously sings!

Beauty on the Wing. When I spotted this butterfly on the wing, I had to pause and catch my breath. It was so stunning. I had my camera, but had to chase it awhile, until it settled down. But I finally got it. This one was photographed along the trail. Later I spotted one on the beach. During the week I camped near Red Lake, I saw several.

This is an Emperor Butterfly I photographed last fall in Northern Minnesota. I just love their velvety, filigreed wings.

The poem is a Faux Limerick.

A limerick is a short, humorous, often ribald or nonsense poem, especially one in five-line anapestic meter with a strict rhyme scheme (AABBA), which is sometimes obscene with humorous intent. The form can be found in England as of the early years of the 18th century.

The standard form of a limerick is a stanza of five lines, with the first, second and fifth rhyming with one another and having three feet of three syllables each (nine syllables); and the shorter third and fourth lines also rhyming with each other, but having only two feet of three syllables. The defining "foot" of a limerick's meter is usually the anapaest, (ta-ta-TUM), but catalexis (missing a weak syllable at the beginning of a line) and extra-syllable rhyme (which adds an extra unstressed syllable) can make limericks appear amphibrachic (ta-TUM-ta). Source: Wikipedia.

What makes this a Faux Limerick is, that I didn't follow the meter requirement, humor aspect, and only 5 syllables in the short line. So it's similar, but not exact.

This photograph was taken by the Author at Washkish, Minnesota, near Red Lake in northern Minnesota in September of 2012.

CHAPTER 6: SCENES

. . . .

"What are Scenes?" you might ask.

For the purposes of this book, scenes are poems based on a photograph that says something. It can be an event, or an image that moves you in some way. The purpose of the poem is for the poet to convey the meaning or feeling that speaks to him. Hopefully, it connects with the reader too in that way.

Poem #35:

CAMPFIRE
(A Pantoum Poem)

Flickering flames in firelight,
Pine logs giving glorious glow
With scented smoke that fills the night,
A twilight camping color show.

Pine logs giving glorious glow
That brightens woodland day's-end scene.
A twilight camping color show,
Sitting around it, so serene.

That brightens woodland day's-end scene,
While roasting hot dogs on a stick.
Sitting around it, so serene,
These are the things that make me click.

While roasting hot dogs on a stick.
With scented smoke that fills the night,
These are the things that make me click,
Flickering flames in firelight.

The season is upon us. I plan to do some of this, very soon.

This poem is a Pantoum

A Pantoum is a poem that is made up of quatrains with interweaving repeated lines. In that sense, the Pantoum is a form of poetry similar to a villanelle. It is composed of a series of quatrains; the second and fourth lines of each stanza are repeated as the first and third lines of the next. This pattern continues for any number of stanzas, except for the final stanza, which differs in the repeating pattern. The first and third lines of the last stanza are the second and fourth of the penultimate; the first line of the poem is the last line of the final stanza, and the third line of the first stanza is the second of the final.

Ideally, the meaning of lines shifts when they are repeated although the words remain exactly the same. So, although they are the same words, their meaning is changed. this gives the poem it's intrinsic beauty.

A four-stanza pantoum is common (although more may be used) and in the final stanza, you could simply repeat lines one and three from the first stanza, or write new lines.

The Pantoum outline is as follows:

Stanza 1 A B C D (or A C B D)

Stanza 2 B E D F (or C E D F)

Stanza 3 E G F H

Stanza 4 G I (or A or C) H J (or A or C)

The photograph was taken by the author at Lake Elmo campground.

Poem #36:

CATHEDRAL ON THE HILL
(A 3X Poem)

Cathedral high on city hill
Set there on the highest hill
Light that brightens up that hill
Keeps the evening sky so still

See it there above my town
Shining jewel that crowns the town
The glow of God lights this town
Like a lovely golden gown

Placed high above the river
Brightly framed by that river
Blesses homes along the river
The sight gives me a shiver

Sparkling glow of shadowed light
Spots the town with beams of light
Water shimmers with that light
A vivid vision in the night

This is a night photograph of the Cathedral of St. Paul at night shot from across the river on the Smith Street Bridge (also known as the High Bridge). The river shown is the Mississippi river. There are luxury apartment buildings along its bank complete with lighted walkways. The rest of the downtown around it is subdued with dotted light here and there. It sits in the highest hill in the downtown St. Paul, Minnesota area.

This poem is a 3X Poem.

This "3x" format was developed by Fanstorian PF aka Pipersfancy.

It has a fixed rhyme scheme of unique repeating rhymes. Although not typical, it makes for an intriguing display.

The end rhyme words of the 1st three lines are the same (Therefore the term, 3x)

The 4th line has to rhyme but is not identical, making each stanza mono-rhyme.

Minimum four stanzas

This photograph was taken by the author himself.

Poem #37:

DANCING WATER
(A Triolet)

Dancing water on clear display
In a pure pool of cobalt blue,
That ripples up, streaming spray.
Dancing water on clear display
In delightful cascade array,
It enhances a garden's view.
Dancing water on clear display,
In a pure pool of cobalt blue.

This fountain is actually in a garden of a condominium complex along the Mississippi River at the Upper Landing area of St. Paul.

This poem is a Triolet.

A Triolet is a poem with a fixed format. This one has a syllable structure of 8 counts or tetrameter. It is a poem of only eight lines with a rhyme scheme of only two rhymes (a and b) that can be represented as follows: ABaAabAB, where the fourth and seventh lines are the same exact line as the first. The eighth line is the same exact line as the second (This is represented by the capital letters shown). So, it is very important to compose the first two lines carefully so that the entire poem flows well and is enhanced by the repeats.

This photograph was taken by the author himself.

Poem #38:

DRIP

Drip

DRIP

Runoff
The melt has begun
as snow
dissipates

Transition takes place
Before
Our Eyes

Regeneration
As new growth
Begins

Rebirth

Buds and Birds
Bugs

New life
and
New beginnings

DRIP

Drip

drip

Spring has arrived. Rejoice!

I know winter is losing its grip, when the snow begins melting off my roof top, as it is here in this picture of the gutters on my house overflowing.

This poem is written in Free Verse.

Free Verse poetry is a very open and free flowing form of poetry written without required formats. There is no fixed meter, tempo, or rhyme. The author, instead, paints a poetic picture with the words. The author adds dimension in how the poem is felt, through the use of pace and pause, created in how the words are arranged on the page. This can create very moving thoughts and images. Done correctly, it can turn simple sentences into lovely works of art.

The photograph is from the Author's collection of his Garage roof overhang. Taken March 30, 2013.

Poem #39:

LOVE IS FREE

Love is free, enjoy love
Give freely yourself and Give
Shove away doubts, so gently Shove
Live magic moments … you'd fondly Live
Share secrets you thought you would never Share
Love is free, enjoy love
Dare bravely, show without shame what you Dare
Above those fears conquered, rise Above
Care to open the door with Care
Live to Love … Love to Live
Love is free, enjoy Love

Love is free

Just kind of playing around, experimenting with this structure and rhyme. Sort of complex and not sure I like it, but let me explain.

There is double meaning to this poem. It can be taken for intimate love between two lovers, or as Spiritual love. The door to the soul, or the door to the church and God's love.

Each line begins and ends with the same rhyme word, so the poem rhymes on both the left and right side, except for the 3 syllable refrains. Just the main Stanza

It begins and ends with the 3 word refrain about love, which also starts the first , middle, and last lines of the main stanza which contains 11 lines.

Syllable count and rhyme scheme is pretty complex.

Syllable count is: 3, 6,7,8,9,10,6,10,9,8,7,6,3.

Rhyme scheme is: a bcbcdbdbdcb a

Not sure if this format actually exists, I just thought it up on my own

The photograph is of an Episcopal Church off Dale Street in St. Paul Minnesota. This will become part of my Picture Poem collection.

Poem #40:

MY SACRED SPOT
(Quatrains with Couplets)

Campfires and coffee in brisk morning air,
My wandering wishes take me right there.
Lazily leaned back in my camping chair,
There's nary a note of worldly despair.

In my sacred spot
Where people are not.

I listen to birdsong while making meals,
Squirrels scurry with nuts for Winter's ordeals.
The changing leaves give an Autumnal feel,
Where this sylvan setting is so ideal.

In my sacred spot
Where people are not.

I see Geese formations in azure sky,
As Ducks in their vee go flying by.
I see an Eagle that's soaring on high.
Impressions of grandeur have filled my eye.

In my sacred spot
Where people are not.

Everyone needs one. In the Autumn they are even better.

This poem is simple 3 Mono-rhymed Quatrains with 3 rhyming couplet refrains.

This picture was taken by the author in Northern Wisconsin.

Poem #41:

RAIN FILLED CULVERTS
(A Sonnet Echo)

The rain filled culverts now have waterfalls
That splash and crash and dash about the pond,
A sight of strength and charm of which I'm fond.
When raging torrents turn between stone walls,

A loud cascading cacophony calls.
Cold water rushes freely over rocks,
While tossing stones about like tumbling blocks.
When raging torrents turn between stone walls,

A vortex wave exists that spins and sprawls.
When worldly troubles leave me feeling raw,
It lifts my soul aloft in stunning awe.
When raging torrents turn between stone walls,

The rain filled culverts now have waterfalls
When raging torrents turn between stone walls.

Recent heavy rains have filled the lakes and streams to overflowing. I went over to a local park, and found a usually quiet culvert, that carries a small creek into a pond, had turned into a waterfall with raging waves. Thus I was inspired.

This poem is an Echo Sonnet. I was introduced to it by Gungalo. This is my first attempt at one.

ECHO SONNET: This is a relatively new form devised by the well-respected English Poet, Jeff Green. It takes its shape from three envelope quatrains and a couplet, the last line of each stanza is a refrain that links the quatrains and gives us a rhyme scheme of:

A, b, b, A1, a, c, c, A1, a, d, d, A1, A, A1

Where the first A sets the A rhyme and repeats once in line 13. The A1 of line 4 matches the rhyme set in A, but is a distinct repeating line that echoes 3 more times in lines 8, 12 and 14. This type poem, then, has 4 rhyme sets of A, b, c, and d.

The Echo Sonnet is based on French repeating forms, but unlike those forms which are normally syllabic, the preferred rhyme scheme is Iambic pentameter, or similar, and being a sonnet it should be presented as a 14 line poem.

I took this photograph looking across the pond with my zoom lens on my Kodak 981 camera.

Poem #42:

REVERENCE
(A Free Style Poem)

When evening comes
A pall will fall on all

The birds
Alight
For the night

As
The light of day
Is drawn
Away

God's creations
Bow

and

Pray

All God's creations, even plants and animals feel His vibrations.

A Free Style poem is a subcategory of Free Verse. It is unstructured as to meter and form, but does contain rhyme.

This picture is a Goldfinch bowing its head as if in prayer as the plants around it do so too. The photograph was taken by the author at twilight.

Poem #43:

SUN WORSHIP
(A Pantoum)

~ ~

The Forest is nourished by the Sun
As God smiles down on His Creation
All living things, Yes, Every one
Exists at the Creator's invitation

As God smiles down on His creation
In Deep forest the Tree Tops are high
Exists at the Creator's invitation
Trees cradle the Sun, low in the Sky

In Deep forest the Tree Tops are high
Taking Holy Heat through bending Bough
Trees cradle the Sun, low in the Sky
That worship as the Ancients allow

Taking Holy Heat through bending Bough
The Forest is nourished by the Sun
That worship as the Ancients allow
All living things, Yes, Every one

~ ~

Even Nature worship's the Sun that God placed in the heavens to nourish our planet.

Capitalization is Poet intended

This photograph was taken at Mounds Park in St. Paul Minnesota, the site of Native American burial mounds. The Indians consider it as sacred ground. When I viewed this photograph, it made me think of trees holding up the sun, almost in worship. That caused me to write this poem.

This poem is a Pantoum.

A Pantoum is a poem that is made up of quatrains with interweaving repeated lines. It is composed of a series of quatrains; the second and fourth lines of each stanza are repeated as the first and third lines of the next. This pattern continues for any number of stanzas, except for the final stanza, which differs in the repeating pattern. The first and third lines of the last stanza are the second and fourth of the penultimate; the first line of the poem is the last line of the final stanza, and the third line of the first stanza is the second of the final.

Ideally, the meaning of lines shifts when they are repeated although the words remain the same. So, although they are the same words, their meaning is changed. This gives the poem its intrinsic beauty.

A four-stanza Pantoum is common, (although more may be used) and in the final stanza, you could simply repeat lines one and three from the first stanza, or write new lines.

The Pantoum outline is as follows:

Stanza 1 A B C D (or A C B D)

Stanza 2 B E D F (or C E D F)

Stanza 3 E G F H Stanza

4 G I (or A or C) H J (or A or C)

This photograph is the reason that this poem exists, it moved my Muse to express what I saw in verse.

CHAPTER 7: SUNRISE AND SUNSETS

· ·

This is an area that would own the heart of any poet or photographer. What is more moving than a lovely sunrise or colorful sunset? The beauty and emotions that these release have been the topic of many a bard through the centuries. Many a sonnet has been penned by poets under the spell of these celestial events. Artists and photographers alike revel at the opportunity to capture one.

Poem #44:

BAND OF GOLD
(A Monorhyme)

The sky was captured in a Band Of Gold
Worldly wonder to bewitch and behold
When nature's colors delight and unfold
As the hours ebb and the day grows old.

I was out and about on lovely evening. The sunset lit up the sky in gold across the clouds. I photographed this sky on winter's eve in January 2012 from a scenic overlook of the Mississippi River valley. The picture inspired me to write this 4 line verse.

A little Monorhyme in a delightful sky.

A Monorhyme is a poem that uses the same rhyme across all lines. This one is a simple quatrain in pentameter (or 10 syllables).

This photograph is the reason that this poem exists, It moved my Muse to express what I saw in verse.

I am including it in my book called Picture Poems, which are all poems resulting from the picture image

Poem #45:

THE CREATOR'S COLORS
(A monorhyme)

With an Artist's touch He paints the sky
With a new set of colors for the poet's eye;
With a pastel pallette using painter's dye,
He creates the perfect present as the day's "Goodbye".

I was on vacation in September 2012 on the shore of Lake Bronson State Park

in far northwestern Minnesota, nearly at the Canada border,

when I saw and photographed this sunset.

It moved me to write this small but heartfelt poem.

This poem is another mono-rhyme. The meter is variable in this set.

This photograph is the reason that this poem exists, It moved my Muse to express what I saw in verse.

I am including it in my book called Picture Poems.

Poem #46:

EVENING PRAYERS
(A Quatern)

With setting sun, Earth sings its evening prayers
All living things give blessings for the day
As nightingales break out their song in pairs
The flowers stretch to drink the last sunrays

As dusk creeps in, the worship soon begins,
With setting sun, Earth sings its evening prayers,
And crickets play their leggy violins,
God's creatures pause, relieving daily cares.

The eagles soar, to float on evening airs.
The waterfowl seek quiet place to rest.
With setting sun, Earth sings its evening prayers
Before the world may best lay down to rest.

All gather now, with sunlight nearly gone,
On fragile sphere each organism shares.
They feel the natural cycle moving on.
With setting sun, Earth sings its evening prayers.

Do plants and animals feel a union with nature? Does the Earth itself feel something as the sun sets across its face? Sometimes I feel that they do feel something.

This picture gave me a feeling of peace akin to worship. It moved my Muse to create this poem as one of my picture poem collection pieces. It was taken in January 2011 at Mounds Park in St. Paul, Mn.

This poem is a Quatern, a French poem format with four quatrains that uses the refrain in the first line of the first stanza, as the second line of the second stanza, the third line of the third stanza, and the last line of the fourth. It is usually written with an 8 syllable count per line, but I have modified it to use 10, so that I could also practice doing iambic pentameter. I think I succeeded.

Poem #47:

MORNING MISTS
(A Pantoum Poem)

As morning mists were kissed by sun,
To my delight the flock took flight
On golden veil that heaven spun,
A sign that said, "The World is right".

To my delight the flock took flight.
The fog gave depth to Earth's tableau.
A sign that said, "The World is right",
When sunbeams danced as Starlings flew

The fog gave depth to Earth's tableau
As burst of life filled morning sky.
When sunbeams danced as Starlings flew,
My soul took flight with them on high.

As burst of life filled morning sky,
While fog displayed what God has done,
My soul took flight with them on high,
As morning mists were kissed by sun.

A flock of Starlings take flight from the reeds in Southwestern Minnesota as I marvel at the sight.

I was camping at Blue Mounds State Park in Southwestern Minnesota, and was out for an early morning walk, drinking a cup of coffee. As I approached the riverbank on a foggy morning, a flock of Starlings burst from the reeds and took flight around me. It was amazing to behold. This Poem is about that moment when nature transforms into art.

The Poem is a Pantoum.

A Pantoum is a poem that is made up of quatrains. In a Pantoum the second and fourth lines of the previous stanza are repeated as the first and third lines of the next stanza. So you achieve a tumble of repeated phrases that cascade through the poem. I really like the results this format creates when you can multiply your thoughts and slightly transform them in each stanza. The resulting rhyme scheme becomes abab.

There is no requirement for a specific meter. For this poem I chose iambic tetrameter. I also repeated line one as the last line, but that isn't necessary.

This picture is one of my most acclaimed photographs. Of the 800 photo's I have posted on the web site Capture Minnesota, this one ranked number 3. It was taken in August, 2012 at Blue Mounds State Park, where I went to capture pictures of the Buffalo herd and rare birds in the area.

Poem #48:

POETIC WORDS
(A Nonet Poem)

When I see the wonders in the world,
When I encounter Nature's best,
Beautiful words fill my head.
Just like sweet symphony,
As my Muse moves me
Poetic words
Fall freely
Off my
Pen.

Things of nature can set it off, my Muse.

This is a Nonet Poem, done in non-rhyming free verse.

A nonet is a nine line poem. The first line containing nine syllables, the next line has eight syllables, the next line has seven syllables. That continues until the last line (the ninth line) which has one syllable. Nonets can be written about any subject. Rhyming is optional.

There is no limitation to the number of words per line. Only syllables per line. This provides a great deal of flexibility.

The picture is one I shot in July 2012. Took the photo as I was driving in my convertible with the top down. Of course. I pulled over to take the shot.

Poem #49:

RISING LIGHT
(A Lantern and Cameo Poem)

Light
Beacon
In darkness
Shadows going
Gone

Daylight
On the horizon
Peeks with promise of a new day.
Morning bright,
Shine heated harmony on me!
As you rise high in the sky,
I smile!

Let the sun shine on me. Blessed with another day.

This has two styles of poem, a Lanturne and a Cameo. Both are similar, as being short free verse formats with fixed syllable counts, but different in their structural impact.

The Lanturne is a five-line verse shaped like a Japanese lantern with a syllabic pattern of one, two, three, four, one.

A Cameo is a more rounded style consisting on 7 lines with a syllable count of two, five, eight, three, eight, seven, two. This mimics a cameo's oval shape.

This photograph is one taken by the author.

Poem #50:

SUNSET ON THE LAKE

Rich reflection of the sunset
Floats upon the surface.
As shoreline turns to silhouette,
Night exerts it purpose.

The day is done,
And as the sun
Dips slowly into night,
The clouds drift by
In evening sky,
Reflecting scattered light.

It's at this time, quiet solitude
Exerts a peaceful calm,
That creates the most restful mood,
Befitting of a psalm.

Where moments spent
Make stress relent
To perfect peace of mind.
The world can tell
That all is well,
A wish for all Mankind.

Just another sunset

I came across this format last night when I reviewed a poem of Sandra Mitchell's named - I'll Live in the Sky. It was a beautiful poem in this format. First stanza has a rhyme pattern of, abab. Then the second one is aabccb, alternating throughout. Tempo is: 8686 then to 446446, alternating, to make a lively cadence. This is repeated at least twice.

I'm not sure if this is an existing known format, but if not, it should be named and Sandra given credit. At any rate, I liked it, and used it here.

This is another of the pictures I took one night (5/19, 2013). It is the same sunset that I used on Fire in the Sky, only earlier. Taken at Lake Phalen in St. Paul, Minnesota, while on an evening drive with my wife.

GLOSSARY OF POETRY TYPES